NANUQ

A Baby Polar Bear's Story

Executive Producers, John Christianson and Ron Berry
Illustrator, Lara Gurin
Art Director and Book Designer, Eugene Epstein
Writer and Creative Director, Kathleen Duey
DVD Mastering and Editor, Stephanie Carlson
DVD Soundtrack and Song Composed and Produced by George Fogelman
DVD Audio Mixed and Mastered by Robert Cartwright and George Fogelman
DVD Video Narrator, Daniel Krasner
DVD Song, Sung by Ian Brininstool and George Fogelman
DVD Video Footage, the British Broadcasting Company
Production Manager, Doug Boggs

Distributed by Ideals Publications
A Guideposts Company
535 Metroplex Drive, Ste 250, Nashville, TN 37211

ISBN # 9780824918187
Printed and bound in China

NANUQ

A Baby Polar Bear's Story

It was a perfect spring day.

Soft, fresh snow covered the sea ice.

The bright sun wouldn't go down until September.

My brother nudged me, trying to get me to wrestle.

Suka always wants to wrestle!

My mother was busy
sniffing at the air.
I knew she was hungry—
we all were. She was trying
to find the scent of seals
on the wind.

My mother started walking, and we followed her on a long trek across the snow. When she made a hissing sound, I wasn't sure why she was uneasy. Then I spotted the walruses. She always stayed away from them. If they thought we were trying to steal their food, they would get angry.

My brother and I play a lot.

I like to run and slide in the soft, new snow.

Suka loves to wrestle and race—and he usually wins.

One warm day, my mother swam to a new place. She went slowly so we could keep up and she stayed close to the edge in case we got tired. The seawater washed against the pack ice, splashing and sighing.

My mother finally spotted some seals.
Suka and I had to stay absolutely quiet and still while
she was hunting. It was very hard.

Suka wanted to play, but I knew we couldn't.

We had to watch. We needed to learn how to hunt!

After we ate, Suka and I lay down to nap. Our mother lay down with us, making a rumbling, purring sound.

It snowed and the wind rose. We didn't mind.

The drifted snow didn't make us cold, it helped keep us warm.

We slept for a while...then Suka woke up.

My mother and I wanted to keep napping. Not Suka. First he nipped my ear. Then he sat on me. Then he nipped my other ear.

I finally jumped up and wrestled with him.

We rolled and slid and growled like grownup bears.

Suka held me down and pretended like we were fighting.

I knew he wouldn't really hurt me, but it still made me angry.

I wanted to nap, not play.

The next day, our mother started off as soon as we woke up.

She walked fast, and she kept sniffing at the wind.

We crossed some rocks. I was used to walking on snow.

The smooth stone felt strange beneath my paws!

I wanted to explore and practice searching for scents in the air, but Suka kept trying to get me to play instead.

After a while we were thirsty!

My mother found a thin place in the ice. I hoped Suka
would break it so we could drink the melt-water underneath,
but he just stood there. So I did it, slamming my paws
against the ice, over and over.

There was enough water for all of us. Then Suka wanted to wrestle!
I growled at him. I was tired from breaking the ice.

My mother rested a little, then started off again.
We had to hurry to keep up. She headed for the water and
I wondered if we were going to swim.

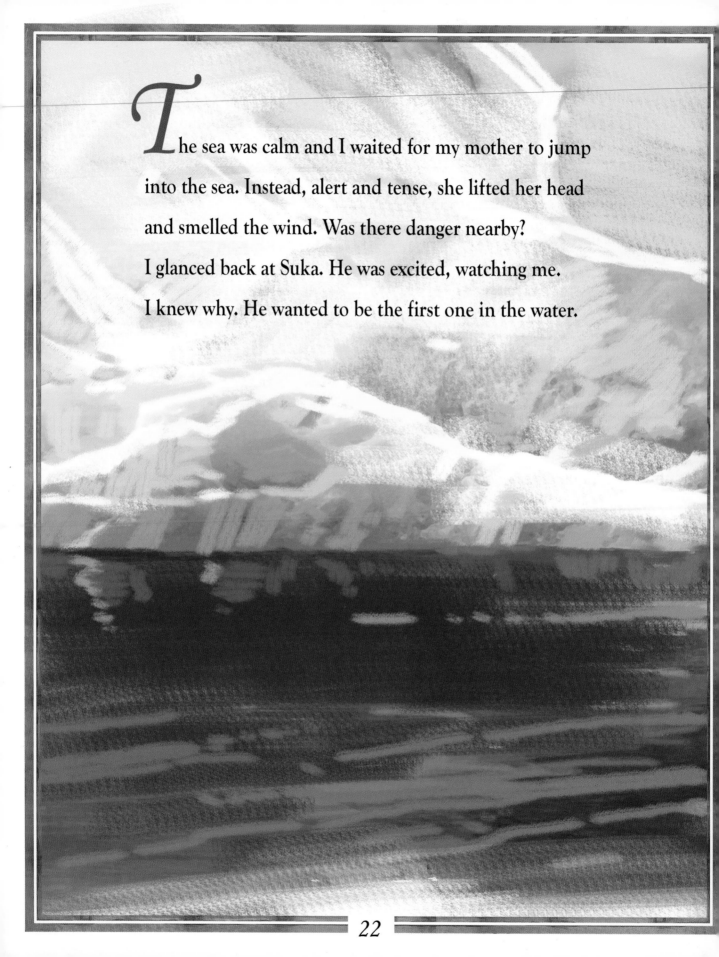

The sea was calm and I waited for my mother to jump into the sea. Instead, alert and tense, she lifted her head and smelled the wind. Was there danger nearby? I glanced back at Suka. He was excited, watching me. I knew why. He wanted to be the first one in the water.

My mother looked down into the rolling waves.
I leaned forward as far as I could and spotted walruses
swimming underwater. Suka must have thought
I was about to dive into the sea. He leapt off the ice pack.

The walruses surfaced, startled and angry.

One climbed onto the ice, but the other one swam toward Suka.

It roared! I jumped into the water behind my brother

and nipped his heels until he surfaced.

When Suka finally saw the walruses, he whimpered
and turned back. Our mother was growling, ready to protect us.
I growled, too. Then Suka did. The walruses swam away
as we pulled ourselves out of the water.

Suka was quiet as we followed our mother across the ice. He didn't try to race me and he didn't bite my ears to get me to wrestle. Instead, he scented the air and helped watch for danger.

We curled up, snuggling close to my mother.

I knew we were safe because she would protect us—

and I would help her. So would Suka.

We were both growing up.

The My Animal Family project was created by a team of people who care about children, their own, and yours. We want to help kids learn about themselves, their families, and their world.

The Illustrated Book

Our beautifully illustrated books are written with care.
Each story is about the realistic adventures of a wild baby animal
and is an accurate portrait based upon current behavioral research.
Every story gives parents and grandparents opportunities to talk to
their children about home, life and family.

The Activity Website

The *My Animal Family* creative team includes game and website designers, too. We have built a **safe**, fun place for kids to play "animal" activities online. At **MAFKidsClub.com**, children will find their favorite animal friends in their native habitats. Set in arctic snow, tropical forests, oceans and deserts, the games help pre-readers get ready for school and keep beginning readers happy and busy. Games are leveled so that each visitor can build confidence and master basic skills. The creative team has worked hard to make the website friendly, fun, interesting, and safe for your kids.

The Live-Action Animal DVD

Every book includes a live-action DVD that features **award-winning BBC** wildlife video footage. Carefully edited for young children, the footage gives them a glimpse into the reality of each baby animal's life. Kids learn about the cooperation that helps animal families survive and thrive, and about the habitats where they live.

MY ANIMAL FAMILY®

LEO
A Baby Lion's Story

Leo goes exploring, then has to find his way back to his family.

KOROW
Baby Chimpanzee's Story

Korow learns to climb high enough to pick her own fruit.

ELLA
A Baby Elephant's Story

Ella helps protect a newborn baby elephant in danger.

NANUQ
A Baby Polar Bear's Story

Nanuq saves his bossy brother from a foolish mistake.

Welcome to the Club!

My Animal Family is a new kind of children's club. With books to read, DVDs to enjoy, games to play, puzzles to solve and adventures to share, it's the kind of club every child dreams of... *"where the fun and good times never stop."*

Membership begins with the purchase of a beautifully illustrated storybook. Every story in the series is captivating and stars a baby animal in a realistic, family adventure... animal families that include elephants, lions, chimpanzees, polar bears, and many more...

Use the secret passcode on your membership card to explore *www.MAFKidsClub.com*. There are no advertisements or fees.